# Becoming a Mentalist
## Unlock the True Potential of Your Subconscious Mind

STEFAN CAIN

Although the author and publisher have made every effort to ensure that the information in this book was correct at press time, the author and publisher do not assume and hereby disclaim any liability to any party for any loss, damage, or disruption caused by errors or omissions, whether such errors or omissions result from negligence, accident, or any other cause.

# DEDICATION

This book is dedicated to my wife, who has encouraged me to write and has proven to me that anything is possible through the power of intention and belief.

This page intentionally left blank.

# CONTENTS

This page intentionally left blank.

# ACKNOWLEDGMENTS

Sincere thanks and gratitude is extended to the following authors who have helped me to understand how nervous systems works, many of whose quotes are referenced through this book:
Mastermind of the nervous system, Tony Robins,
Author of "How to Stop Worrying ad Start Living", Dale Carnegie
Author of "The Power of Focus", Jack Canfield
Author of "Your Erroneous Zones", Wayne Dyer
Author of "Return to Love", Marianne Williamson

1

## Introduction

Did you ever notice how some people just seem to light up a room when they enter, even if surrounded by strangers? It's not a gift; it's a skill. This is the kind of skill with which the mentalist is equipped.

### *What is a mentalist?*

Some people tend to perceive a mentalist as a person with strange supernatural powers. They have the ability to read other people's body language and establish an instant rapport, immediately appearing popular in the eyes of others. The mentalist appears to be able to read minds magically. And, of course, those are the kind of people who find themselves surrounded by friends.

Although many perceive the mentalist as one with supernatural powers, nearly anyone can acquire these skills by having discipline and learning a few basic tricks. You too can access different types of human illusion simply by reading this book. However, keep in mind that it's important to practice these exercises as you go along. The human body has a feedback mechanism that is geared for excellence, and this mechanism is constantly changing and evolving to help you achieve excellence.

Whenever you encounter feedback that indicates that you're doing something right, you're intrinsically geared to steer yourself in that direction. Feedback from other people indicating that you've taking a wrong turn, however, will send you back to try again. It's important not to give up, but to build on what you've learned to continue to do better. Obviously, if you don't practice these exercises with other people, you will not have the opportunity to grow your skills.

### *The following pointers will get you thinking like a mentalist:*

- **Smile at others.**

Did you ever notice that when you smile at someone, they smile back at you? This actually works with practically anyone, including babies and people of all cultures. It's a universal sign of joy. And not only does the simple smile make others around you feel better, it will actually make you feel better too.

Your body and how you feel both physically and emotionally can be dictated by the simple physiology of how you carry yourself as well as your body language.

Try it out on yourself. Spend one minute looking at the floor, and you will notice that you're starting to feel depressed. Now spend a minute looking out at the world and smiling – even if no one is there. You'll start to feel extremely happy. The science behind this is that facial expressions such as smiling have a distinct effect on brain activity, causing the person to feel how their face indicates they feel. In fact, some studies even reveal that smiling helps the body to experience less pain.

Smiling is a simple trick that actually tricks the brain into feeling good.

- **Take an honest interest in others.**

I do not mean to pretend an interest. You need to truly decide to take an interest in the lives of your friends, family and co-workers. Not only will you find that work has become more interesting, but you'll see how people suddenly will want to befriend you.

If you can stay open and curious about others, you will become a friend magnet.

*"You can make more friends in two months by becoming really interested in other people than you can in two years by trying to get other people interested in you. Which is just another way of saying that the way to make a friend is to be one."* **… Dale Carnegie**

No one likes to be judged. Once you change your outlook and take an honest interest in the lives of others, people will subconsciously feel the acceptance and be more open with you.

You might be thinking that you have no interest at all in your colleague's life. However, this is only *your* perception based on what you believe or know about him currently. Once you decide to become curious, you might discover interesting things about your colleague that will change your perception.

Think about something that has changed your outlook in the last year. Perhaps a new TV show that you never thought you would have wanted to see ten years ago is now your favorite. If you're not curious by nature, it's a good idea to work at this to make it a lifelong habit.

- **Live your life in the present.**

*"If you're feeling depressed, you're living in the past; if you're feeling anxious, you're living in the future; if you're feeling at peace, you're living in the present."*... **Lao Tsu**

This is so true! Think about it. Whenever you're feeling down, take note of your thoughts. What are you thinking? Most likely, it's something about the past that is impossible to change (or so you believe).

And what are you thinking about when you're feeling that burst of anxiety? Most likely it's something about the future about which you're feeling uncertain. "Will enough money come in time to pay my bills?" "Will I be able to make it into work on time?" Thinking thoughts such as these will not help you. Becoming anxious about what might happen will only put you in a state of fear and close your mind to being aware of possibilities. And the more you focus on worry, doubt or fear, the more fearful you will become.

- **Look for things to amuse you.**

When you can find things to laugh at, you're keeping yourself in a light and open frame of mind. It might be difficult at first, but try not to take everything so seriously. Did you ever pass by a happy child and wonder what it would be like to have no worries? I thought about that the other day when I passed a child giggling and skipping, and then looked at his mother who had a depressed look on her face. Being amused with life is natural for us. Unfortunately, we teach ourselves to feel depressed and anxious as we grow into adulthood.

We have been conditioned throughout our lives to look past the fun possibilities and find potential danger. It's time now to recondition us to thinking like a child again. Realize that your need to be right comes from your ego, not your true self. Meditation helps to calm the body and put things in proper perspective. Whether your troubles are a mere challenge to make life interesting or an earth-shattering catastrophe, the choice of how you perceive them is up to you.

- **Assume rapport.**

    When you meet new people, imagine that this person is your new best friend. Taking on the habit of feeling relaxed and seeing amusing things in others will help you with this. This makes conversations less awkward and more enjoyable. And that's easier for both you and the other person.

As you dive into the material in this book, keep these five pointers in mind and practice them daily with the people in your life. Notice the difference in how you feel and how others treat you, and write down any changes you see. You will be amazed at how you are actually becoming a mentalist-minded person.

# Chapter 1
# What is a Mentalist?

We all know that guy, the one with the charisma who seems to turn heads just by walking into a room. And he's no doubt successful as well, right? What's his secret?

Actually that word, "charisma," is sourced with the definition "gift of grace." In modern times, it has come to imply a compelling attractiveness that inspires devotion in others, and, more recently, a mysterious elusive quality (Wikipedia, 2016). Don't you get rather excited when you witness this kind of person?

Some think that these people who seem to magnetize success are magicians. Some call them clairvoyant, and some even believe they have supernatural abilities.

Contrary to popular belief, a true mentalist is different from a magician in that they use the power of their mind to create illusions. The confusion lies in the fact that mentalists seem to be able to create magic, although not all magicians are mentalists.

Magicians simply learn a magic trick and demonstrate that trick. Even children are capable of doing that! But the true mentalists have a way of playing mind games on people they don't know, using their knowledge of how human nature responds to questions. A magician with mentalist abilities is an illusionist – the man who has the power to make something real seem to disappear into thin air. In reality, the disappearance act is only in the perception of the audience. The mentalist is aware of human perception and knows the exact capacity of the human brain.

A couple of well-known illusionists today are David Copperfield and Chris Angel. These performers, while having attained a skillful knowledge of the human mind, are still considered to be illusionist magicians.

Of course, some entertainers such as David Blaine and Dynamo perform with both magic and illusion.

Are the performers mentioned above mentalists or magicians?

Bottom line, illusionist magicians such as David Blaine do perform tricks that make them look like mentalists. However, the true mentalist possesses a specific set of skills and understanding in psychology.

*So exactly what are the skills that the mentalist dominates?*

- **Memory techniques– knowledge of advanced procedures of how to remember details**

There are a lot of tricks of the trade for memory. For example, the mind palace technique is a skill you can train yourself to do over time.

In a nutshell, using the mind palace to remember a list of objects means to simply build a sort of palace in your mind. (This is best to do before trying to remember your items.)

Once you can imagine different rooms and hallways in your mind, the idea is to metaphorically place the object in that room in your mind and attach an emotional response to the item. For example, if you want to remember to pick up bananas, you can picture hundreds of bananas in your mind's kitchen, dancing naked as they peel off their skins. This elicits an emotional response when you think about the bananas and, therefore, is imprinted in your brain as a solid memory.

Of course, this particular technique takes time and effort to perfect.

However, it has been said that some people can actually memorize an entire deck of cards by using this memory technique.

- **Knowledge of Body Language**

Although we are all different with unique personalities, the amazing fact remains that we still all seem to possess universal body language – gestures such as hands to the mouth indicate telling lies (contrary to the popular belief that the eyes tell lies). An example of this is portrayed with the 88 times Bill Clinton brought his hand to his face when defending his honor in the Monica Lewinsky episode.

Conversely, open hands when speaking are an indication of an honest person. However, beware of a speaker who continuously speaks with open hand gestures, as this could be an indication of a skilled liar. Consider the hand gestures of Donald Trump with open hands out on a continual basis. Perhaps he's telling the truth, although he could just as well be an experienced con man. And whether he's actually telling the truth or not, his poll numbers have reflected that the average person does subconsciously buy into the open hand body language.

- **Ability to Profile a Personality**

The mentalist is skilled in the ability to size up an individual's personality and character simply by observation. The skilled mentalist has the ability to let go of any preconceptions or emotional biases. They are able to teach their super-senses to look deeper than the normal layman looks to access intuitive insights. Of course, anyone's senses can be taught to be super-senses, given enough discipline.

- **Magical Deception – the ability to deceive what the human eye can see**

They say the hand is quicker than the eye. This is the truism that gives the illusionist the benefit of the doubt. But the mentalist takes this a step further with seemingly impossible actions using a completely natural process.

Keith Barry has the skill of mentalist abilities down pat by using what he calls brain magic, which is no more than mind reading effects with the proper knowledge of psychology. Illusionists will create the illusion of a sixth sense; Barry, on the other hand, has a way of manipulating the human mind with his performance tricks. He speaks of second sight, where a mind control expert and see through the eyes of someone else. "Magic is all about directing attention", Keith explains when expounding on how he was able to drive a car blindfolded.

- **Hypnosis – Ability to plant a hypnotic suggestion in a seemingly normal conversation**

The mentalists use what they call awake hypnosis where the power of suggestion is used without the person knowing. Derren Brown uses suggestion cold reading by guessing what people are thinking by suggesting "it starts with a P, doesn't' it?" Neuro Linguistic programming (NLP) is now a widespread technique used among marketers to plant ideas into the buyer's mind that he wants to buy the item for sale.

- **Ability to show off the skill – the mentalist has a way of capturing the attention of everyone around him**

By definition, mentalism is referred to as a performing art, which demonstrates highly developed mental or intuitive abilities. This goes without saying that a mentalist is a performer.

Of course, we can all strive to attain the mentalist's skills without being an entertainer. However, it's the ability to show off and capture the audience's attention in the first place. After all, what good is it to attain a skill such as mentalism if you have no means by which to demonstrate it?

As performers go, mentalists are currently "in," as opposed to the old-fashioned magician with his bag full of tricks. People are amazed and mesmerized by the mentalist who performs the impossible right before our eyes. Of course, truth be told, he has enough knowledge of human psychology to be able to predict our responses.

We all find that fascinating, and rightfully so. We know it's not really magic, but how is it done? Or rather, what exactly are we missing as we observe?

On the surface, it appears that the mentalist must be a clairvoyant or mind reader. However, the truth is that anyone can attain these same skills with a little knowledge and discipline.

***Just begin your venture with the following steps:***

- **Practice quick judgment.**

The mentalist has the ability to carry himself with aura of confidence. Practice trusting your own instincts and making confident judgments. You can size up a person quickly by asking yourself:

a) Is this person looking into my eyes?
b) Does this person appear healthy, as though he takes care of himself?
c) Is this person showing signs of anxiety such as sweating?


You'll be surprised how correct your initial instinctual responses can be.

## Chapter 2:
## How Can Becoming a Mentalist Change your Life?

Whether you're in for the long haul of actually becoming a whole-hog mentalist, or you're after simply learning a few tricks of the trade, this venture is well worth your time. The abilities of a mentalist reach far beyond performing tricks on stage.

Life is challenging, and the average person will sometimes tend to hide his head in the sand and pretend that the challenges don't exist. Admittedly, this might help for a little while. However, if you continue this type of behavior, you're going to crash and burn.

Look at any successful person and what do you see? Success is the result of making the correct choices in life. Conversely, anyone who has not attained success has made poor choices somewhere along the line.

***What lessons will you learn to equip you to face life's challenges head on?***

- **Learn to stop denying the truth.**

Consider the following life challenges and ask yourself how you might respond:

1) You've been diagnosed with an illness.

Most people might think, "Why does this always happen to me?" This type of thinking adds fuel to your life's crash and burn.

It takes a strong mind to admit that perhaps you might not have been taking proper care of yourself. Once we learn to start thinking about what we might have done to bring this situation on, we now have the power to change life's circumstances.

2) You've just been served a court summons for an unpaid bill.

Do you think, "Those greedy bastards – now they're charging me double the amount of my debt with interest they don't deserve."

That type of thinking will lead you into trying to avoid the situation, perhaps even ignoring the court date and accepting the consequences of a judgment, leading to liens on your home, garnished wages, or even freezing your bank account. This, needless to say, will give you much greater problems than simply appearing in court or getting the help you need to fight the debt.

The advanced mind will perceive this situation differently. Once you can stop denying the truth, your mind will come up with a variety of innovative ideas and ways to get the debt paid down without adding more stress on your life.

3) The love of your life wants to break up.

Do you get on the phone with your best friend and start ranting and raving about the idiot that did this to you? Are you looking for your friend to agree and tell you that you're better off without the person?

That's what psychologists call rationalization, and it can get you into trouble.

Once you have the ability to take an honest look at yourself, you might be able to see how perhaps you might have been a little too controlling. Marriage and relationship is always a two-way street, yet the average person only sees himself as a victim when challenges such as this arise.

*"If you're gonna make a change, operate from a new belief that says life happens not to me but for me"...* **Tony Robbins**

Once you can teach yourself to accept your own life's circumstances, this gives you new power to change and grow out of the circumstances that have been holding you back, no matter what they are.

- **Learn how to control yourself.**

The people in AA have it down pat: "Give me the serenity to accept the things I cannot change, the courage to change the things I can, and the wisdom to know the difference." This attitude of life is not just a tool to help you stop drinking, it's an attitude that can change anything in your life that you want to change. You don't have to be an alcoholic or even have a belief in God to accept that attitude. People who are the happiest in life have learned to be OK with whatever happens, period.

You may have been born into a dysfunctional family. These days, that's really the norm. Stop blaming your family for your own mistakes. We all have the ability and freedom to make our own choices.

You might have been diagnosed with a terminal illness. While this is not the norm, that illness can eat you alive if you bury your head in self-pity. Conversely, learning to accept your situation offers your brain creative ways in dealing with the situation. Becoming a victim to circumstances in your life is truly a choice you make.

The more you surrender to what you think life is doing to you, the more vulnerable you become, thus opening the door to more despair coming into your life. This opens the door to losing friends, drug or alcohol abuse, and depression.

Once you realize that, no matter what happens, *you* are the one in control of your own life, a healthy support system seems to appear out of nowhere and you're surrounding yourself with good influences.

- **Change the way you look at things.**

An experienced mentalist does this by second nature. Conversely, most of us believe life just happens *to* us, where the reverse is actually true. We possess a power to steer our life's circumstances toward better or worse, based on our attitudes and how we deal with the hand we're dealt.

*"Change the way you look at things, and the things you look at change."* **Wayne Dyer**

Of course, to some extent, stuff does happen that's beyond our control. Life's challenges require mental strength on your part. And if you choose to believe you're a victim and ignore the issues at hand, you're likely to end up with much bigger problems.

Our problems are here to help us grow, thereby enabling us to become stronger. Once you can learn to control your attitude, you'll learn how to control what happens next in your life rather than allowing it to control you.

Seeing the glass as half-full instead of half-empty does not merely mean that you'll feel better about the empty part. It actually has a way of transforming your situation from bad to better, and from better to good.

*"The secret to success is learning how to use pain and pleasure instead of having pain and pleasure use you."*... **Tony Robbins**

Pain can be a great motivator, enabling us to strive for higher goals and to work harder. Many successful people who are now millionaires were once in a state of extreme pain and despair.

- **Embrace your strength.**

Yes, you do have strength within you, and that strength is apparent once you accept where you are, learn to control your responses and change your attitude, with a consistent focus on a positive outcome.

*"You can conquer almost any fear if you only make up your mind to do so. For remember, fear doesn't exist anywhere except in the mind."..* **Dale Carnegie**

As you notice yourself becoming stronger, praise every improvement, even if ever so slight, and watch your strength grow.

- **Realize that you have been your own worst enemy, and decide to befriend yourself.**

We're all human and we all make mistakes. You can't expect that you are any different. We all fall, because it's a fallen world. It's whether or not we make the decision to get up, *and how we do it*, that makes all the difference.

Guilt about one's own mistakes can bring down even the best of us. Be aware of these feelings and push them away. Whatever has happened in the past is the past, and this has no power over your future. The wake of the ship does nothing; it's the engine that keeps it moving forward.

In order to heal and relieve yourself from guilt, you must accept your own circumstances, forgive yourself, and make the best decision you can to get on with your life.

*"Times does not heal everything, but acceptance will heal everything."* ... **Buddha**

Decide to treat yourself as you would your best friend, with acceptance and encouragement.

- **Gain proper perspective of what really matters in your life.**

No one wishes on their deathbed that they had spent more time at the office. Regrets, when put in the proper perspective, make you realize what's really important in your life.

As you become better equipped with your growing mentalist attitude and awareness of others, you can't help but also take a serious look at yourself and your own situations.

Now you're starting to adopt an attitude that brings joy to your life over the simplest things.

# Chapter 3:
## The Power of Focus

Lack of focus remains one of the largest factors in causing hardships. We all tend to become victims of circumstance, which then limits the empowering belief of what is actually possible. Once we learn to focus on our strengths, everything becomes easier. The following steps will help you learn how to strengthen your focus so as to weed out all of life's static that's distracting you and keeping you from success.

- **Create good habits.**

Your habits not only determine your quality of life, but also can dictate your future. If you notice, successful people have acquired successful habits; unsuccessful people have not. So how do habits really work?

Any behavior that you persist repeatedly, either consciously or unconsciously, becomes a habit. Most of us wind up with bad habits because we're simply not aware of those behaviors that become so repetitive that they become habit.

It doesn't take many midnight trips to the refrigerator for your favorite ice cream before you suddenly find yourself unable to sleep without that routine trip.

But let's examine the idea of creating a habit out of something difficult. You probably thought that driving a manual transmission car was difficult when you first tried. However, after you learned how to do so, you didn't even have to think consciously about how to drive at all. It's a habit.

Driving a car is only one example of something that is hard at first and then becomes very easy. Anything is easy once you know how to do it.

The trick is to discover what habits you would like to develop. For example, if you don't have as much money in the bank as you would like and you would prefer to be financially independent, why not develop better financial habits? If you don't have a habit of saving and investing 10% of your income regularly, this might be something to strive for. Remember, to make it a habit, you must remain consistent with your new behavior.

How can you determine what new habits are best for you? Everyone wants a better *quality* of life. Start paying attention to how you think and feel – what do you *really* want? Most people actually can't even answer that question. Reassessing your options on a regular basis is a good habit to develop. From there, you can be better equipped to decide what activities you would like to learn which will later become successful life habits.

The problem with habits and why we tend to accumulate so many bad habits is that most people live for immediate gratification. It's so easy to sign the loan to buy that new car, and the immediate gratification is so rewarding in those first few months. But when you're coming around to year four with those car payments and your car no longer has that sexy glow, the feeling that had once empowered you has now turned to stress.

We need to understand that life gives us consequences, and usually they don't show up until much later in life. Although developing successful habits takes time and effort, up to 47% of our everyday behavior is habitual.

Start becoming aware of what you do habitually and ask yourself what effect that behavior might have on you a year from now. In the beginning, forcing yourself into a new behavior seems difficult; however, after the first three weeks, it becomes much easier. After a few months, your new good habit is practically on automatic pilot.

If you're not sure what successful habits to create to change your life, study a successful role model. Successful people have successful habits. Do they listen well? Do they read a lot? What do they read? Do they belong to any associations? What are their drinking or smoking habits? It could be advantageous to spend time with successful people you know and ask them about how they became successful.

You might notice that people who are successful and prosperous in every sense of the word find joy in learning. They know that there's always another level to reach for, and the feeling of success is in the journey itself. Once you realize that, you can start feeling successful right off the bat.

### *Follow the successful habits formula:*

1) Identify your unproductive habits that could be causing you pain.
2) Define your new successful habit. If you're not sure what it is, just take the opposite of your identified bad habit.
3) Create a 3-part action plan. Action is the keyword here. Nothing will change unless you have a plan to make it change. Write down your new successful habit and list three to things to incorporation in your lifestyle to make the new behavior a habit.

- **Streamline your focus by not multitasking.**

We have major issues that we need to focus on; however, more often that not, we get sidetracked and thus lose the power of focus.

*"Learn how to separate the majors and the minors. A lot of people don't do well simply because they major in minor things."*...**Jim Rohn**

Many of us brag about being able to multitask. In fact, many jobs demand that the ability to multitask is essential to the job.

Contrary to popular belief, studies have shown that multitasking actually limits the amount you are able to accomplish because it limits your focus. The brain in reality only has the ability to pay attention to one thing at a time. People who believe they're multitasking are, in fact, alternating their focus from one activity to another. This has been proven time and time again to be ineffective.

- **Focus on your natural talents.**

Take a look at the successful people who have accentuated their talents. Barbara Streisand never had a nose job. Instead, she took comfort in the fact that the oversized nose she had been blessed with was a great asset to her voice. We often hear her humming in movies, a beautiful sound that would never have been possible with a small nose.

Other women with similar facial characteristics may have taken a different perspective. Some may have focused instead on negative features, thus limiting their awareness of their beautiful voice. They may not have been aware of how the nose is probably a gift to ensure such a warm, magnificent sound. But Barbara knows how to accentuate her positive features. As a result, she not only is known for her beautiful voice, but her beautiful looks as well.

That is not to say that her stardom was a gift with no effort. She was practicing to perfect her voice from a very early age. Once we are aware of our strong attributes, focusing on the positive generates success.

- **If you're feeling overwhelmed, get help.**

As a control freak myself, I can attest to the fact that there's a lot to be said for letting go and letting the universe take over. Controllers typically have a mindset that nobody can do things as well as they can.  This may be true with some things, but nobody is the best at everything.  Take an honest look at your strengths and weaknesses and allow others to help wherever possible.

To take a logical approach, consider how much you're worth per hour and think about the tasks you're taking on.  If you're a trained engineer and your time is worth $260 per hour, you're really wasting your time if you're trying to do your own bookkeeping.  Be willing to allow others to help.

### *Use the 4-D solution:*

1) Dump it (only do what is worth your time to do).
2) Delegate it (ask who else can do this).
3) Defer it (schedule a time later for non-essential tasks).
4) Do it (take immediate action for the most important tasks).

- **Develop clarity.**

When it comes to focus, clarity is everything.  It's impossible to focus on anything if you're not clear on what you really want.  People who are successful are able to create pictures of the future in their mind.

You might think it's just a waste of time to spend time daydreaming about your desired future.  However, most successful people have done just that.  Think about things in your life that you *have* successfully accomplished.  How much time did you spend pondering about it?  For many of us who have successfully accomplished our goals, we found ourselves pondering this dream with complete clarity every waking moment.

*"The future belongs to those who believe in the beauty of their dreams."*… **Eleanor Roosevelt**

When it comes to clarity, use the following guidelines to ensure that your dreams are worth manifesting:

1) Your goal must be something *you* want, not the wish of someone else.
2) Have a clear intention of *why* you want what you want.
3) Your goals must be specific and measurable. (Instead of saying you want more time with your family, specify how much. Instead of saying your goal is financial freedom; specify how much you intend on making.)
4) Keep your goals flexible. (A flexible plan allows you freedom to change course if a better opportunity comes along.)
5) Your goal should be challenging and exciting. Ask yourself how you feel about acquiring your goal. If you feel excited and can't wait to get started, you're on the right track.
6) Your goal needs to be in perfect alignment with your values. If your deepest values are working against your future dream, you're on the wrong path. For example, if your dream is to make a million dollars with online marketing, but you subconsciously believe that you're stealing from strangers to make a buck, you'll be only wasting your time.
7) Your goal should be integrated and well balanced. Make sure you include time in your dream for having fun and enjoying the finer things in life.
8) Set realistic goals. This is not to say that any goal fired with enough desire and intent is unrealistic. It's only unrealistic to believe that you can make a million dollars in a short amount of time. Make sure that the plan to achieve your goal is realistic.
9) Your goal should include contribution back to society. Not for them, for *you*. When your focus is on others, then all your needs are taken care of for you. When you can give unconditionally to others, your payback will come in unexpected ways.
10) Your goal should be supported. Selectively share your dreams with a few people you trust.

*"If you go to work on your goals, your goals will go to work on*

*you. If you go to work on your plan, you plan will go to work on you. Whatever good things we build, end up building us."* … **Jim Rohn**

# Chapter 4
## Becoming Aware of Your Environment

Most of us, whether we know it or not, spend almost half of our day running on autopilot. Have you ever envied someone who seems to have the ability to observe the slightest details and possess an extreme power to focus? We all have that power within us if we choose to develop it.

Becoming more observant is an asset to you in various ways. Once you've developed your observation skills, you'll find yourself with greater ability to focus without getting sidetracked, hence increasing your job performance. Additionally, better awareness will make you smarter with the sensitivity for more fulfilling relationships.

***How can you improve your own power of observation? The following activities will help you in developing these skills:***

    1.  Use mindful meditation to increase awareness.

At first blush, this would appear to be counterproductive. How can you be more aware of your environment when you've got your eyes shut, closing out all exterior noise?

On the contrary, once you can perfect the skill of how to clear your mind, this also gives you the ability to clear out the superfluous life static that surrounds us. The average person gets distracted when state is broken with an interruption. Have you ever been interrupted from what you were doing and you forgot what it was that you were trying to do in the first place? Don't worry, it's not that you're getting older – you're just allowing your brain to get overly distracted.

Developing your meditation skills sharpens your attention and focus – the two most necessary skills needed for observation.

If you've never tried to meditate before, you might find that it's hard to concentrate and your mind will tend to want to wander. Don't worry, that's normal. Just keep working on this exercise by closing your eyes in a quiet environment and focusing on your breathing. Breathe in through your nose and out through your mouth slowly and steadily. Imagine all anxiety leaving your body as you exhale.

Brain scientists have discovered that the brain's grey matter responsible for sensory processing, attention and focus becomes thicker and larger during meditation. As a result, you will be better skilled at memory, focus and attention, all skills needed for greater power of observation.

2. Hone your powers of logical reasoning.

Internet sites offering brain games based on logic can help you here. The AARP site has some interesting and fun games, like the slight of hands game. This requires focus, concentration and observation skills. The more you play, the stronger your skills develop.

Additionally, crossword puzzles are good ways to develop the skill of logic. It has been noted that many US Presidents have taken the time to work on crossword puzzles. While you might be wondering how a President could possibly afford that kind of free time, the truth is that using techniques such as this to sharpen your logic skills work to your advantage in getting more accomplished.

3. Develop memory skills.

Contrary to popular belief, a good memory is not a gift. Anyone can develop a powerful memory through the practice of memory activities.

An easy way to get your brain fired up with memory skills is to try to remember a day's event from the previous day or a few days prior, bringing to mind as many details as you can. Make this a game to try to remember more things each time you play.

Another fun memory game is to try to remember your dream when you first awaken. This is not only a great help to sharpen your memory skills, but it can also give you some insight as to your innermost thoughts.

For the advanced student, the mind palace is a great way to sharpen memory. This is a technique used by advanced memory students where you picture your mind as a familiar place with several doors, and rooms – perhaps your home or office building. The place, called the palace of the mind, should be extremely familiar to you.

Each thing you are attempting to remember is placed in your mind in a different palace compartment. Because you're putting this strange thing in a familiar place, you're more likely to remember it. Attach an emotional memory to the thing, and it's in your mind for good. Some extremely experienced mentalist professionals actually have the ability to memorize an entire deck of cards with this technique.

    4.   Observe new environments and pay attention.

Many of us are subject to tunnel vision because we're stuck in a rut. 47% of our actions are ruled by habit; we take the same route to work every day, we execute the same routine every morning and every evening. Very often our minds are held hostage by thoughts about our day – worrying about the day ahead, or regretting how the day went in the past.

What can we do about it? Try to experience new things by taking a different route or trying out a new place for lunch. And then, really immerse yourself in the experience, taking in every detail.

As you focus more on your surroundings and really try to remember details, you're now living in the present.

*"Do not dwell on the past, do not dream of the future, concentrate the mind on the present moment."* ... **Buddha**

Think about it: The past is gone and thinking about how things could have been done differently will only torment you. The future is not here yet and there is no guarantee of what tomorrow brings, which also introduces an element of stress and worry. When you can focus on your life as it is in the present moment, then the prefrontal cortex of the brain is free from stress, thereby enabling it to become stronger.

Psychologists have found that focusing on the present strengthens the mind-body connection, which makes for a more productive life. The point here is that when the body is caught up in thinking about how things should have gone in the past or what to do to change the future, a stress response is created. That portion of the brain caught up in stress is now non-functional and depletes the ability to focus.

The more we can train our brains to focus on the present moment, the less stress we'll have, and that in itself increases the ability to focus on any project at hand. Try paying attention to as many details you can in the present moment, then later test yourself to see what you can remember about the event.

5. Learn to observe through taking notes.

Many well-known book authors keep a note pad with them at all times so as to take note and remember good ideas that come up throughout the day. You can check yourself by looking at a room and trying to remember all the details. Then look again, writing down things you observe in a room. After you have the list, look back again at the room and see how many things you can notice.

You will find that you can remember many more details after you've written them down. Handwriting has a more positive effect on remembering as opposed to typing. Once you write things down, you're more likely to remember.

***Once awareness has become a habit, greater habits can be developed.***

As you become more aware of yourself and your feelings, you can begin developing more awareness as to the actions of others.

Now you have the understanding and awareness of your own body language, and it's time to start being aware of the body language of those around you.

# Chapter 5
## Reading Body Language of Others

While the mentalist appears to possess mind reading abilities, the real secrets of those abilities lay in the ability to read the body language of others.

For example, most of us have been lied to at one point or another. Wouldn't it be a refreshing change to actually have the ability to know when someone is lying to you or being deceptive?

In the previous chapter, I made mention of becoming more aware of your environment and your own personal feelings. Let me now suggest that, as you're aware of your feelings, you look in the mirror and take note of your own body language and particular gestures you make.

Although we're all different, most body language is as universal as the smile. The unconscious microexpression works on a principle called the ide motor response, an expression in which the person producing the expression is completely unaware. Although this is a universal response, some people are more vulnerable than others.

### *What are the facial body language tricks for the mentalist?*

- **Microexpressions**

The mentalist is aware of microexpressions, the fundamental expressions we all use based on the six universal emotions. Learning these basic expressions will enable you to recognize feelings in others, making you a better communicator. Additionally, you will also be able to be more aware of your own feelings.

Microexpressions are completely involuntary, and these telltale expressions are the most widely used among mentalists. These expressions take practice in noticing, as they will normally only last 1/15 to 1/25 of a second. Unlike extended conscious facial expressions, the microexpression cannot be faked.

Microexpressions actually happen when a person is hiding his or her own feelings from themselves. This can be either conscious (repression) or unconscious concealment (suppression). A person who is put in a situation where he would want to conceal his feelings generally exhibits microexpressions.

The ability to recognize microexpressions has actually proven to be more effective in lie detection than the popular lie detector test. The reason for this is that the traditional lie detector test recognizes only anxiety – now *why* the person might be anxious.

An example of this is brought out in an episode of the TV series *Lie to Me* where a 16-year-old boy was almost imprisoned for life because he exhibited feelings of anxiety from a lie detector test when asked about the woman who had been killed.

His microexpressions, however, gave more insight into the situation. He did in fact exhibit feelings of anxiety; however, those anxious feelings were due to a sexual attraction that that he had been taught was wrong in a Christian upbringing.

The expression is briefly revealed on the person automatically before he has a chance to suppress the emotional response.

Dr. Paul Ekman, researcher for the TV series *Lie to Me* has succeeded in a groundbreaking technique of decoding the human face.

These revolutionary studies conducted by both Dr. Ekman and Dr. Friesen revealed that anyone could actually see microexpressions with the proper training.

He teaches that there are seven categories that are easy to detect in the human expression:

1. Fear

The fear microexpression is revealed with eyebrows raised and drawn together. Only the upper eyelids are rising, and the mouth is open with lips tense or drawn back.

2. Anger

This microexpression is illustrated in the TV series *Lie to Me* where the killer had an expression of score on his face when the correct place where the bomb could be found was mentioned.

You'd think that killers would not reveal the same emotional expressions as normal everyday people; however, this same facial expression was found on the face of Dick Cheney.

Anger expressions show bulging eyes, lips pressed together and lower jaw pointing outward. Even the body language expert Donald Trump cannot hide his anger microexpression in some of his speeches.

3. Happiness

Alternatively, the happiness microexpression is also expressed on the same killer's face when the wrong place is mentioned and he is trying to conceal his happiness with the wrong guess. It is illustrated as an ever-so-slight turn up of the corner of mouth for only a brief instant.

4. Sadness

Sadness is the hardest expression to fake. It is revealed with the eyebrows drawn in and up, and slight downward movement on the corners of the mouth and lower lip pouting outward.

5. Surprise

Want to know if your friend is truly surprised by your gift? Watch for the slight signs of eyebrows raised and curved, with eyes widened enough to show the white above and below. The jaw is dropped open with teeth apart. A fake surprised expression would probably be held longer than a genuine surprised expression.

6. Disgust

The contempt, disgust or hate expression reveals one side of the mouth raised. George W. Bush is known for this expression.

7. Shame

The microexpression shame is illustrated with the hand brought to the head and eyes facing down. This expression was witnessed on the face of President Clinton during the Monica Lewinsky trial.

Practice feeling the above emotions; watch yourself in a mirror and witness for yourself what these expressions look like.

Of course, keep in mind that the microexpression is an unconscious expression and therefore happens in only a split second. It takes a lot of practice to become skillful in noticing the expressions in others.

It's interesting to note there that additional research by Dr. Paul Ekman reflects that, when we try to mimic a microexpression, we initiate a psychological experience of that emotion.

- **Macro Expressions**

Macro expressions are also subconscious but easier to spot, since they can last one half to four seconds. Macro expressions often are repeated and in sync with the sound of the person's voice.

These expressions occur spontaneously with individuals; it's a natural expression that occurs, but the individual is aware and does not try to conceal it.

Dr. Matsumoto, professor of psychology in San Francisco, conducts workshops for people who want to learn more about how to interact with people face-to-face by reading emotional cues in a clinical setting. His work shows that all facial expressions are universal with no bias towards face, culture, gender, age or religion.

It is also interesting to note that a person who may have been blind from birth will also exhibit the same expressions as anyone else.

- **Subtle Expressions**

Subtle expressions measure the intensity of an emotion and can be detected when the individual is just starting to feel an emotion. Additionally, a low-intensity emotional response to a situation is called a subtle expression.

There is a high correlation between recognizing subtle expressions and detecting deceit. A new study now suggest that subtle expressions are actually more powerful than microexpressions in observing whether or not someone is lying.

How are subtle expressions different from microexpressions?

When the person is just beginning to feel an emotion, a subtle expression can be detected.

The ability to spot a microexpression has to do with how quickly you notice a split-second emotional response. Conversely, detecting subtle expressions enables you to recognize how a person is feeling from picking up on subtle expressive hints, such as variations in expression. For example, a slight tightening of the lips might indicate a concealed sign of anger.

Microexpressions form across three regions of the face. When expressions appear in less than all three regions, this is called a subtle expression. Subtle expressions come and go just as fast as microexpressions and are even more difficult to detect; however, they are just as valid. Expressions indicating loss of control or intent to harm will generally appear longer on the face.

Obviously, the above categories are only the tip of the iceberg when it comes to reading human emotion. The human face has 44 facial muscles capable to creating over 7,000 different expressions. However, there are only a few facial expressions you'll need to be able to read in order to detect how a person is feeling.

- **False or Masked Expressions**

As if it's not enough to learn expressions to decipher the emotions of others, we also have to deal with the human tendency to hide their emotions.

Many people throughout history have faked emotions for various reasons.

*"You can go a long way with a smile. You can go a lot farther with a smile and a gun."* … **Al Capone**

There are several reasons why people try to act differently than how they feel; the need to hide emotions in an effort to stay professional to keep your job is common. And, of course, there are always some people who choose to be polite and don't want to let on how miserable they really are.

Real happiness can be detected by looking at the eyes. The muscles on the outward side of the eyes tend to wrinkle up a bit with a real smile.

Sadness is actually more difficult to fake. The facial expression should reveal drooping lower eyelids, corners of lips pulling downward and eyes losing focus. Actors and people who are successful in faking sadness find that if they do fake this expression, they will actually begin to feel real sadness.

While any expression can be faked, as done with professional acting, it is actually impossible to fake microexpressions, which is why they are now becoming popular with people involved with investigations and law enforcement.

### *What about other parts of the body?*

Involuntary gestures of hands also give us great insights into the minds and emotions of others. Since most people tend to use their hands as a form of expression, the hand is a tremendous telltale when it comes to reading involuntary gestures.

- **Hand Gestures:**

1. Palms of the hand up and open signify honesty and submissiveness. This can also indicate confidence. However, beware; this gesture can be easily faked and can often be seen with the hand gestures of politicians.
2. Palms hand down with the forearm moving across the body is a sign of defense.
3. Hand over heart is a sign that the person is seeking to be believed. Beware on this one – it's easy to fake!
4. Finger pointing is aggression. You've probably been taught as a child not to point – and for good reason. Pointing your figure signifies aggression and threat. This is read subconsciously on the same level as pointing a gun.
5. Finger pointing and wink means acknowledgement and confirmation. The exception to the finger-pointing rule is pointing and winking- this brings a totally different connotation. When someone makes a remark you like, you

may respond with a finger point and wink as a confirmation ditto of the remark. It's as if to say, "You got it".

6. Finger pointing in the air symbolizes power. You might notice that Donald Trump uses this gesture a lot. Experienced speakers who want to be heard with emphasis on their message use this gesture.

7. Finger wagging means warning or refusal. You see this on the hands of moms giving warning to children.

8. Clenched fists signify anger. This could also signify resistance or determination and needs to be taken into context, as many gestures do.

9. Fingertips and thumbs touching signify complex thinking and thoughtfulness. This is another favorite gesture you'll often see on Donald Trump as he speaks. This is a good gesture to remember when giving speeches, as it tells your audience you wish to engage connection. And beware on this – it's also another one that's easy to fake.

10. Knuckle cracking is usually done by males and is an attention-seeking habit. The person doing this may be insecure as he strives for attention.

11. Touching nose while speaking is a strong indicator of lying or exaggeration. People often make this subconscious gesture when embellishing the truth or when telling an outright lie. Also, nose scratching is a warning sign (unless of course the nose is genuinely itchy). Take note of these gestures wisely. Pinching or rubbing the nose while speaking is an unconscious signal of a wish to suppress what has just been said.

12. Hands touching the ears signify rejection to something heard. It's as if the body is saying No, I don't want to hear that." This is an indicator that your listener disagrees with you.

13. Scratching the back of the neck is a strong indicator of doubt and disbelief. If you're talking and someone is scratching their neck, perhaps they don't believe you. It's also a subconscious indicator for a person's own disbelief – indicative of not telling the whole truth.

14. Running hands through hair is a flirtation signal. While this sign usually means the individual is flirting with you,

beware, as it can also be a sign of intense irritation or annoyance. It is necessary to read other facial clues to decipher true feelings.

15. Hands on the hips indicate confidence. You'll see this stance most likely in sports situations, with the individual is emphasizing presence and readiness.

- **Other body telltales**

Your entire body is communicating on your behalf whether you're speaking or not. Additionally, consider the following body postures and look to see them in others:

1. Feet pointing outward could mean a person is anxious to leave. If you witness someone sitting with their feet pointed in a different direction, this is a strong indicator that they are anxious to leave.
2. Toes pointed inward are signal of insecurity.
3. Fidgeting signifies tension. You might catch yourself doing this from time to time. Tapping your toes, scratching the arm of your chair, crossing your legs and bopping your foot up and down all are ways of relieving tension. And, of course, all of these body language signs can be observed from others. If you notice someone fidgeting, they're probably tense or stressed in the present situation.
4. Even leg crossing can give away inward feelings. Take note of which direction the top leg is pointing. That's generally the direction toward the person they feel is most approachable. And, there's more – if the toes point up in that direction as well, this is an indicator that they have positive feelings toward that person.

Take note of ways in which people are standing, sitting and their facial expressions and see if you can decipher what they're feeling.

# Chapter 6
## Neuro-Linguistic Programming

Neuro-linguistic programming, or NLP for short, is often used among professional businessmen and sales experts as a way to manipulate one's response. Of course, mentalists and conmen are experts as well on this recently discovered technique.

The NLP expert has the ability to influence brain behavior (neuro) through language (linguistic) and other types of communication. This actually rewires the brain to respond to stimuli (programming) in a different way. As a result, the desired behavior is manifested.

This type of brain programming often incorporates hypnosis and self-hypnosis to achieve the desired change. While most people think of hypnosis as a way of putting someone into a trance, as some TV shows may suggest, the truth is that we all are hypnotized in several different ways. Marketers use hypnotic language to get you to want what they're selling. Authors use hypnotic language to get you interested in the book. As you read this book, you are probably unaware of other things around you, which is a form of being hypnotized.

While the ability to read body language signs can help you determine a person's feelings, the real trick is to now manipulate the individual to act in the way you desire – the way that NLP experts can predict.

### *The origin of NLP:*

NLP was created specifically to allow us to magically predict the behavior in others based on an understanding of both verbal and non-verbal communication. The NLP expert has the ability to recognize how a person's basic communication is affecting his brain. As a result, fundamental knowledge of NLP helps us to communicate more effectively with others as well a to gain control or our own instinctive reactions to life experiences.

John Grinder, a linguistics expert, and Richard Bandler, a mathematics and configuration expert, originated this phenomenon.

Their original studies in 1975-76 distinguished verbal and behavioral patterns of therapists Virginia Satir, family therapist, and Fritz Perls, gestalt therapist. Gestalt therapy focuses on insight into perceptions in subjects and how it links to what they see. This therapy often uses role-playing to aid in resolving life struggles.

Later in the 1970's, the studies expanded to study verbal and behavioral patterns of widely accepted clinical psychiatrist, Milton Erickson, founder the American Society of Clinical Hypnosis.

### *NLP encircles the three most influential human senses:*

1. Neurology

Our nervous system controls the mind, which determines how our bodies function.

2. Language

Language determines how we communication with others

3. Programming

Programming illuminates the essential flow between mind and language.

When learning NLP, one opens the door to self-discovery, as it provides the basis of understanding the human experience.

### *What can knowledge of NLP do for you?*

- Enables you to be a clear thinker
- Helps you in managing your thoughts, which reflect in your moods and behavior
- Enables you to communicate more effectively with others
- Increases efficiency in your skills

### *First, let's study the mind:*

We first need to accept that we can never *really* know reality. Everything we look at and think about is only our *perception* of what we see. You might see a rainbow and think about its majestic beauty; someone else might look at the same and not see the rainbow but rather only a miserable rainy day.

*"The only difference between a flower and a weed is a judgment."* ... **Wayne Dyer**

The way in which we experience life is through our own sensory perceptions. The perception of our experience determines how we behave. The more we can widen our perceptions of what we see, the better we can make the right choices in life. Wisdom is the result of the ability to achieve multiple perspectives.

A more perceptive person is skilled in whole brain thinking. Most of us go through our daily routines in a sort of tunnel vision. The more we can promote whole brain thinking, the more aware we become.

### The following exercise will help you in promoting whole brain thinking:

1. Write in cursive the alphabet a few times. Be sure that your handwriting flows continuously, writing, not printing. Think about how it flows as you write.

2. Now use your opposite hand and do this exercise again with your non-dominant hand.

3. Using your dominant hand again, write the entire alphabet again a couple of times.

Continue the above steps, alternating hands until you feel like the letters can write easily flowing with both hands. This usually take about five times changing hands.

While this exercise might sound silly, the idea is that it has the ability to ingrate language with creativity, which strengthens both sides of the brain.

Memory exercises help as well, such as the mind palace technique mentioned in chapter one. There are also a number of games online geared for strengthening memory.

**Language study:**

Once you have a grasp on being aware of a person's feelings through body language, it's time to allow language to do its magic. The linguistic part of NLP is the art of communicating in such a way so as to manipulate the person's thoughts to result in changed action.

Marketers are using hypnotic language all the time when they attempt to sell the *feeling* rather than the item. Take note of the next commercial you see and ask yourself how it makes you feel. Do they display jeans and talk about the stitching? Or, do they show you tight fitting jeans on a sexy body enjoying life? People who watch the commercial are sold because they identify with the fun feeling, and they are convinced that buying the jeans will give them a fun life.

There are several types of persuasion tools with NLP language, but the there are five vital language patterns for which NLP focuses:

1. Reframing

It's all about perception. Whenever you witness any situation, it's how you perceive the situation that creates your thoughts, which in turn create your actions.

This is one of the most useful NLP techniques. Whenever you're trying to get a friend to see a different point of view, you're reframing by explaining your perception. If you slip and fall on a banana peel, you probably won't be laughing, although others watching you might laugh as they perceive it differently.

The process for reframing is to first identify the action you would like to change. Ask yourself what positive change would you like to make. For example, if you would like to get your teenaged son to pick up his clothes, offer communication that will elicit good feelings. Put yourself in your son's place.

The realization that nagging won't work can be brought home by imagining how inspired *you* would be to mow your lawn more often if your neighbor is constantly complaining. Positive communication attached to memorable feelings brings lasting change.

2. Presuppositions

Presuppositions are the part of your sentence that is assumed. The person listening tends to unconsciously believe the assumption, as the sentence would not make sense otherwise.

Persuasive language is developed when you use distortions or generalizations in your language. These are presuppositions. It's natural to believe that which others assume of you. Marketers will often successfully close the sale with words like "*when* you decide to buy" rather than "*if* you decide to buy". This type of language presupposes that the customer will *want* to buy. Of course, once they buy, they are completely convinced it was their own idea.

Experts use presuppositions in language with deliberate intention to change one's perception.

### 3. Double Binds

This is a hypnotic language technique useful to sales people and those who have a need to persuade others. The technique creates an illusion of choice, which in turn increases cooperation. You've no doubt heard this type of language from a salesman. "Which credit card will you be using?" or "Are you paying with cash or credit?"

The choice technique is also successfully use by some parents; "Would you prefer to take the garbage out before or after dinner?"

The person whom you are persuading is subconsciously assuming the presupposition because they're distracted with making another choice.

### 4. Embedded Commands

This is another sales trick done in both speech as well as website sales copy. The trick here is to embed the words you want your customer to remember by repeating it in a different context. An example of this is "*By now* you should understand the benefits of this product." The embedded words *by now* are subconsciously perceived as *buy now*.

Additionally, this technique can be implemented with voice inflection and/or body language. If you want your friend to calm down and explain her problems, you might say, "I'm here when *you're ready to talk*." When the words "*you're ready to talk*" are spoken, you might say those words slower with a hand motion.

It's important to remember that all embedded command sentences need to spoken as commands, spoken with a decisive confident voice. Using the same words with your voice up at the end sounds like a question and infers hesitation.

Once you have accomplished reading the body language of others, the above language techniques are quite effective in changing perceptions of the other person. As perceptions change, thoughts are changed, which, in turn, changes actions.

# Chapter 7
## The Art of Finding Lies

Your knowledge of hypnotic language can be extremely effective; however, if you're unable to tell if someone is lying to you, then any ability you may have learned is completely null and void. And everyone lies at some point or other, from preschoolers on up to senior citizens.

It would be a true skill indeed to be able to tell when someone is lying. But how can you? Over the years, lie detecting machines have been used among a wide variety of facilities, from corporate employers to FBI agents. However, contrary to popular belief, it has recently been discovered that the traditional lie detecting machine is actually not as accurate as a skilled human lie detector.

A machine has the ability to detect anxiety, which is a major emotional response from anyone who is withholding the truth. However, the machine cannot tell *why* the person is exhibiting anxiety. Telling a lie is only a small portion of the cause of anxiety.

However, being a human lie detector is extremely difficult. In fact, since everyone is different, there is no way to indicate deception 100% of the time. Lie detecting actually calls for examination of multiple behaviors and analyzing these behaviors within the frame of reference for the situation.

Having said that, there are some easy telltales that can give away when a person is feeling uncomfortable and, hence, could possibly be lying.

Psychologists have found that people use a type of body language as a pacifier when they're feeling stressed, and these pacifiers are common ways to see if a person is lying. The object here is to see if the person is feeling uncomfortable because most people do feel stressed and uncomfortable when telling a lie.

*The following body language pacifiers are universally common among humans:*

- Rubbing the back of the neck

- Pursing lips
- Face touching
- Fidgeting – playing with jewelry or small object
- Covering eyes
- Hand wringing

Since different people use different pacifiers to ease stress, it often takes a little getting to know the person first. Mentalists will often ask a question to the subject that they already know is a lie and observe behavior.

Once the pacifier is spotted, the game becomes easier. Mentalists who claim they can choose under which cup the coin is hiding simply look at the subject's body language. When that pacifier is displayed, the mentalist seems to magically know where it had been hiding. Of course, all focus is on the subject's body language, not on the coin under the cup.

### *Look for congruency in detecting lies:*

We all know the language of sarcasm, yet many of us have never given it any thought as to how we can decipher a sarcastic sentence from a serious one. It all has to do with congruency between body language and words spoken.

For example, if you hear someone say, "Yeah, he's really got it all together," and at the same time you notice eye rolling, you're aware that it's a sarcastic remark.

Detecting lies also has to do with discovery of congruency between body language and verbal language. If someone is telling you that they had a wonderful time at your party and you notice that their body language is not in sync with their words, it's likely they're lying.

We naturally use our hands for emphasis when explaining something truthfully. Take note if you observe a person not using any body language and simply speaking the words. This is a sign of incongruence and giveaway of a potential liar.

### *Look for synchrony in detecting lies:*

Synchrony is the connection between the words spoken and the emotions given the circumstances of the event. For example, there was a couple that claimed their toddler had claimed into a hot air balloon and called the police for a wild chase. You could see on the parents' faces that they were not genuinely hysterical, as anyone would be in the case of a runaway balloon with child. We later had learned that the boy appeared out of the attic where he had been hiding.

Simple head movements are also signs of synchrony. If the mouth doesn't match the body, it's most likely that it's the body that's telling the truth. Some people actually shake their head no as they're stating yes. Needless to say, this is a dead giveaway.

### Look for instinctual behavior in detecting lies:

Humans, much like animals, also have a tendency to freeze with little or no movement when feeling stressed. As animals will freeze in motion when experiencing fear of being observed, humans sometimes also freeze based on this same instinct when in fear of being caught in a lie.

### Notice the palms of the hands in detecting lies:

While it has been mentioned in the body language chapter that showing the palms of the hands is a sign of honesty, beware of the person showing palms up all the time. Some political speakers of our time make sure their palms are up most of the time during the speech – another liar giveaway.

### Check out the lying eyes:

Eyes are a huge giveaway when it comes to lying. Contrary to popular belief, if a person looks you square in the eye, this is not necessary a sign that he's telling the truth. Most liars do look you in the eye when lying.

So what *can* the eyes tell you?

The direction of the eye is very important. Eye directions are universal signs, and most people are totally unaware about the direction of their eyes.

**Take note of the following eye directions and their meaning:**

- Eyes up and to the left: visual remembering

This is a sign that the person is trying to remember, which is a sign of telling the truth. Eyes look up when trying to visually remember. Try it on yourself: ask yourself what color was the house where you grew up. Your eyes will unconsciously move up and to the left, (which appears right others).

- Eyes up and to the right: visual creativity

When a person looks up and to the right, it's a sign of creating the visual image. Therefore, beware of a person looking up and to the right, as they would be making up the story as they go along.

- Eyes straight and to the left: auditory remembering

Just as up and to the left signifies a visual memory, straight looking left indicates remembering a particular sound. Remember your baby's first laugh? What did your eyes do?

- Eyes straight to the right: auditory creativity

This is also a sign of creativity. Just as looking up and to the right indicates trying to make up a visual story, straight and to the right is an indicator of creating an auditory constructed sound. Try to image what sound an animal would make if a dog were crossed with a cat. That's when you're looking straight right.

- Eyes down and to the right: kinesthetic remembering

When we reminisce about how an experience made us feel, we're looking down and to the right. Try remembering how you felt the last time you warmed your hands by the fire. Your eyes will roll down and to the right.

- Eyes down and to the left: internal dialog

Although some may not want to admit it, we all talk to ourselves in the form of thought. When we're thinking these thoughts of internal dialog, our eyes roll down and to the left.

What do these eye directions have to do with lying?

Eyes turning right can potentially signify a sign of deception. As a rule of thumb, people do tend to look to the right when making up stories, either auditory or visual. The exception to this is eyes turning down and to the right, as this depicts remembering a feeling.

There are, however, exceptions to the eye rule:

- Left-handed people tend to have opposite eye directions.
- Looking straight ahead as if in a daze is also a sign of visual accessing.
- Use eyes as a lie detector tool in conjunction with other behaviors and body language. We are all different.

### *Other facial lying signs:*

The lying eyes must also be taken into context with other parts of the face. The following indicates other indications of deception:

- Raised eyebrows

A lying face will generally reveal inner eyebrows appearing upward towards the forehead's center. Similar to the eye right direction, the eyebrows can seal the deal.

- Lips will turn down

The sides of the lips turning downward can be an indicator of fear, which reveals a possible liar. It's actually more difficult for the liar to control this response than any other facial response. It's often detected as a microexpression by an experienced mentalist.

- Facial touching

This one is the easiest to spot. It's a common response for a person who is not telling the truth to touch their nose or mouth, as if the subconscious mind is trying to cover the mouth to avoid telling the lie.

The above body language signs are actually indicators of what the brain is trying to accomplish:

- The frontal lobe of the brain subconsciously warns the body that the truth does not want to be told.
- The right side of the brain is stimulated to create a different story.
- The brain is concentrating on how to come forth with the lie without appearing deceptive
- The brain is trying to analyze the listener's response to see if they are buying the lie.

With all of the body language signs of lying, what we need to remember is that the signs are indicative of emotions of stress and nervousness. After all, most of us do feel somewhat afraid at the thought of being caught in a lie.

However, that's more of a giveaway for a generally honest person. It is possible for a dishonest person, or worse yet a psychopath, to prevent the common telltale eye movements. These are dangerous cases, since people who are skilled in preventing the signs of lying are also in effect convincing themselves of the lie.

The signs do, however, reveal emotions of most average people on a universal level.

# Chapter 8
## Decoding Non-Verbal Communication

Non-verbal communication is a universal language that is revealed on a subconscious level among all humans around the globe. While body language is a huge portion of what can be detected on a non-verbal level, the definition of non-verbal communication goes even further.

There are also unspoken presuppositions based on how a person acts. For example, if you're in the middle of a business meeting with a potential client and the phone rings, it's not a good idea to interrupt the meeting. This is screaming non-verbally to your client that you would rather talk to someone else than listen to him.

The same goes, of course, in regards to having dinner with one person and texting on your phone at the table to another party. It goes beyond rude – it's a strong indicator that you don't care that much for the person you're having dinner with. Therefore, it poses a potential friendship loss or termination of business rapport.

Professional mentalists have the ability of decoding all kinds of non-verbal communication – something you will be learning in this chapter.

*Let's discuss ten rules of thumb for decoding non-verbal communication:*

    1.   Learn to observe details in your environment.

This is rule one of becoming a mentalist. Mentalist or not, the habit of being aware of the world around you opens the door to success on so many levels.

While our ancestors were keen in observing potential environmental survival risks, those of us in today's world are more focused on making ends meet in a completely different way.

You'd think that technology would make us more inept in working smart; but the result is many of us wind up working harder. We're torn in so many different directions, and we think that multitasking to get several things done at once is the answer.

Contrary to popular belief, multitasking is actually in effect holding us back. Additionally, it's the cause of stress in so many lives as we march through life trying our best to keep all plates up in the air without letting anything crash.

In a world where we find ourselves surrounded by laptops, cellphones, television, and radio, it's definitely a challenge to focus on one thing at time. However, studies have shown that those who consider themselves expert at multitasking actually get less done in the long run. The science behind this is that your brain actually can only *really* focus on one thing at time. So if you think you can successfully text while you're driving, what you're *actually* doing is allowing your brain to toggle between two different things. And, each time you toggle back, you lose time again while your brain is refocusing to gain perspective. Try turning off outside noises and disruptions while you're working on a project and see how much more you accomplish.

As for being aware of your environment, if you're not distracted with making your brain toggle between three different things at once, you're more likely to notice little details such as microexpressions on faces or inconsistencies in body language.

    2.   Observe others in context.

Observing in context has to do with looking for inconsistencies. For example, if a mother claims she has lost her child, you would expect her to act quite hysterically, with perhaps signs of shaking or shock.

When at work, take note of your colleagues in the work situation. Tune into a political argument and take note of body language. Watch for signs of anger or frustration. Observe persons of opposite sex with non-verbal communication. Are they acting appropriately with focus on work? Once you gain practice in people watching, it begins to be fun. You can begin to predict what people are thinking and how they might respond.

3.   Watch for universal nonverbal signs in human behavior.

As you observe conversations, watch for microexpressions and nonverbal signs of truthfulness. This can get to be quite fun as well once you start getting good at it. It's fun to watch the facial expressions and hand motions of politicians or news anchorman as they talk. If they're making mention of a recent tragedy, do you notice microexpressions in the face that indicate true feelings? What are their hands doing? Some politicians continue to show palms up all the time – a sign that something is not right.

Hand gestures and facial expressions should be in context with the subject matter being spoken. A genuinely sad person will show a sign of true melancholy in microexpressions. You will note that hand movements are in sync with facial expressions.

4.   Watch for idiosyncratic nonverbal behavior.

93% of the meaning of what is being said is transmitted nonverbally. This is why we detect sarcasm. If someone says sarcastically, "Yeah, he's really intelligent", we know from their facial expression whether it's a serious remark or not. No more than 35% of the meaning of any communication is transmitted through words. Nonverbal behavior is idiosyncratic to a large degree. That is, although certain expressions are universal in nature, they vary from person to person.

Some people might purse lips as a sign of anxiety, while someone else might stroke the back of their neck. Still others might experience nervous tics.

5.   Study the baseline behavior of those with whom you
     interact.

Just as each of us has an underlying type of personality, each of us also has a baseline style of acting. Study your closest friends and what appears to be their normal expression. How do they usually sit, and how are feet normally positioned? From there, you can be more adept at taking note of behavior changes based on situational context.

For example, George Bush was known for biting the inside of his mouth, while Prince William was known for patting his head – both demonstrating signs of anxiety.

    6.   Watch for behavior clusters.

Body language appears in clusters – several gestures and expressions, revealing emotions and mental state.  When you can begin recognizing a cluster of behaviors, it becomes far more reliable in mental awareness of others.

For example, if a person is anxious from possibly withholding the truth, you might observe a hand to the back of neck, and at the same time you'll notice eyes rolling up and to their right.  Although anxiety can be linked to various causes, lying or being untruthful is often linked with anxiety.

    7.   Notice sudden changes in behavior.

Impulsive changes in behavior are a strong indication of human emotion. If a person is having difficulty processing an emotional event, a complete change in demeanor can be noted.

For example, suppose a person recently learned that his dog was seriously ill.  You've known this person to have a baseline personality to be cool, calm and collected.  However, today is different; he's showing strong signs of anxiety, noted in his facial microexpressions, faster breathing, or hands brought to the face.

As we become aware of these signals, we become better friends with those around us.  We are no longer caught up in the tunnel vision of our own lives, and we're more likely to ask our friends about what might be their source of trouble.

    8.   The ability to detect misleading or false information through nonverbal signs is crucial.

Since humans are, well, human, we all sometimes have a tendency to hide our true feelings.  The skilled mentalist has the ability to recognize true body language signs of emotion vs. what is faked. This takes a lot of practice and experience to become proficient at detecting false signals.

However, it's good practice and even fun to watch politicians on TV to decipher body language. I say this because when you're watching television, you're able to put more focus on body language as listening to words is less critical as opposed to conversing with someone in person. See if you can notice exaggerated signs that don't seem authentic. An example of this would be palms facing up all the time, as seen by Donald Trump. Additionally, touching hands to heart is a signal demonstrated by George W. Bush. While both palms out and hands to the heart can be translated to a genuine emotion, when exaggerated in speeches, they can be signals of deception.

Another giveaway is when a person is talking with no hand gestures. It's human nature to use our hands as we talk. People who are withholding the truth will sometimes keep hands restrained so as not to give away true emotion.

9. The ability to discriminate differences in behavior as signs of comfort vs. discomfort is elementary in body language observation.

Those with feelings of comfort have no signs of anxiety, revealing facial expressions of happiness and contentment. A genuine relaxed smile will show wrinkles around the eyes. Genuinely happy people are content with their lives and have no signs of anxiety or fear.

Conversely, persons experiencing discomfort are generally anxious, noted with fidgeting, pale face, fast breathing, tense muscles or clenched fists. Speech will vary in tone, sometimes with voice tremors and high pitch.

Depression is also a discomfort feeling demonstrated by a trembling lip, flat speech tone, or slow movements with dropping body.

10. Try to be subtle when observing others.

This is why I suggest first observing persons talking on television or video to detect authenticity. People generally don't like being watched. If you're not good at it, you're likely to be judged back for judging them. If the person is better at reading body language than you are, you're likely to be caught in action.

### *In summary, reading human signals, keep the following pointers in mind:*

- Observe in a place where you can assess the situation with a clear view.
- Take note of pacifier signs.
- Observe signs of nervous or stressful behavior.
- Try to get the person to sit down in a relaxed setting before leaping to conclusions about anxiety.
- Be aware of the person's baseline behavior.
- Once the pacifying behavior has been detected, watch out for increased pacifying signs.
- Ask questions as you observe responses.
- Be sure to ask focused questions that allow behaviors to be revealed.
- Spoken words that can be verified are more likely to be truthful as opposed to senseless chatter.
- Take note of guilty emotional behaviors: Feet pointing outward (a signal the person is anxious to leave), tightening lip or jaw (a signal of stress), and pacifying responses (hands to the face like nose touching, hair twirling, skin picking, moving hands through hair).

Keeping in mind the above Ten Commandments can help you in decoding human behavior, both verbal and nonverbal.

# Chapter 9
## How to Be a Good Listener

While most of this book so far has been covering *nonverbal* body language, there still is much to be said for *verbal* communication. For example, even as an expert in deciphering nonverbal communication, how much of a movie plot do you suppose you'd be able to grasp when watching a move in a different language?

Language is important, yet so many of us listen with half an ear, keeping our own personal thoughts at the foremost in our minds. For example, have you ever been listening to your friend tell a story and you feel your mind wandering? And then, unexpectedly, you hear a phrase that interests you. Now, embarrassed with your tail between your legs, you find yourself asking, "Whom are we talking about again?" Don't worry, it happens to the best of us.

***Don't allow your own feelings to interfere with that which is being said:***

Let me give you an example: The other day, my spouse and I saw a neighbor we had not seen in a while. The last we had spoken to him, we had mentioned having him over while his wife was out of town. The conversation went like this between my spouse, our neighbor and myself:

Spouse: "Hi Charlie, we hope we didn't miss having you over before your wife gets back – when is she returning?"

Neighbor: "She's actually coming home this evening."

Spouse: "Ah, that's too bad, we were hoping to have you over sooner."

Neighbor: "Yeah, I've been eating microwave meals all week, can't wait for a home cooked meal."

Spouse: "Well you can enjoy having your wife home tonight."

Neighbor: "She's not coming home till after midnight, I won't even be up. I need to go to bed early to get up at 3 AM for work tomorrow."

Spouse: "Well, maybe next time we can connect… have a good evening."

I thought that the conversation I had witnessed screamed that our neighbor was looking for a good meal and perhaps we could connect. I would have asked him myself but I wasn't sure my spouse was in the mood for company.

So when I approached my spouse and asked why now have Charlie come over, the response surprised me: "He didn't want to come over, didn't you hear him? He said we missed our opportunity and his wife was coming home this evening."

Conversations such as these are often misinterpreted based on the listener's own personal feelings. My spouse had prejudged our neighbor and believed that he did not want to come over prior to the conversation. Therefore, he heard the conversation entirely different than I what I had heard. I heard our neighbor was begging for a free meal and neighborly fellowship; he heard that he did not want to spend valuable time with us because his wife was coming home and he had to go to bed early.

The skilled mentalist is aware of how preconceptions can skew our listening skills. He looks beyond the vowels and consonants for a clear understanding on the person's thoughts and feelings.

***The following steps will help you in learning to listen deeply by understanding the complete situation of what someone is trying to say:***

1. Be attentive.

This is easier with some people than others. You mind wanders when that guy with the monotone voice starts speaking. But try to look directly into the speaker's eyes and do not interrupt.

In some cases, you might think you know what the person is saying and so you begin to answer by rudely interrupting. You could possibly miss the person's entire point when you do this, as you are interjecting your own personal thoughts without listening wholeheartedly to his.

2. As a good listener, your attention is solely on the one who is speaking to you.

Have you ever been talking with someone only to see how she is looking over her shoulder and watching to see someone else she might know? This happened to me at church one day when I was speaking to a woman I thought was my friend. To my surprise, right in the middle of my sentence, she waved to another person and started talking to someone else. Actions such as these should be taken seriously, as it is impossible to really connect with two people at once and stay truly sincere. It's one reason why I don't go to church anymore.

3. We need to put technology aside and give the human being our full attention.

In our day of high technology, texting while speaking to others is a common mistake that many people make while speaking to a friend or colleague. It's a nonverbal scream that you care more for your phone and perhaps the other person contacting you than you do for the person with whom you're currently speaking.

4. As a good listener, you'll be listening with the appropriate body language.

Lean forward and show the other person you're truly interested. Crossing your arms or pointing your feet outward shows signs that you don't care to hear the story and you're anxious to get away.

5. Try to listen completely without thinking about what you're going to say.

Most people are thinking about what they're going to say rather than truly listening to the entire story. This is being insensitive to the speaker and you could be missing the main point of the story.

6. As a good listener, you'll want to ask pertinent questions.

Rather than saying, "Yeah I had a similar experience" and then make it all about you, instead ask questions pertaining to the story to help the person embellish the story.

7. A good listener shows empathy.

As you listen, allow what is being said to affect you emotionally and share your thoughts through appropriate body language. Honest concern builds lasting friendships and even lasting business relationships.

8. Avoid saying, "I know exactly how you feel."

No one really knows exactly how anyone feels, and it's a rude put-off. Try your best to understand the person's situation without responding in a patronizing manner.

9. A good listener does not prejudge.

This is the mistake my spouse and I made in the conversation previously mentioned. If you approach a person with a preconception of what you believe they're thinking, there is no way possible you'll be able to hear their message accurately.

10. After the conversation, a good listener remembers.

Take mental notes of what has been said so you can reintegrate it again at another time; e.g., "How's your wife doing? Is she recuperating OK?" Of course, the entire purpose of remembering is to share only positive thoughts – *not* for the use of gossip with others.

As you become a better listener, you'll find that others will want to listen to you. They will be encouraging you to speak as your friendships and relationships become stronger.

### *What about speech tonality?*

Although words are important, studies show that only 7% of the actual meaning of a sentence is derived from words alone being spoken. Body language is a big factor, of course, but the tone of your voice also gives away so much.

Speech rhythm is also a sign of anxiety. Those who are not completely honest with their story will tend to memorize their spiel. Hence, the result is that it is delivered in a non-rhythmic way as if it's being read off a script.

Signs of anxiety and guilt are often illustrated with speech tonality and rhythm. A nervous person is likely to be speaking faster with changed pitch, either higher or lower than normal. Body language reveals a dryer throat. This can be witnessed by watching for licking lips or grabbing water.

Additionally, liars might also leave out emotional body language and speak in a more monotone sounding voice. Pronouns are usually emphasized when truthful statements are being made. For example, "I would *never* have had any cause to steal that money."

An untruthful person might also be muttering words so as not to be completely understood. Watch out for people who avoid offering a direct answer to a question. Some politicians are really good at this. You'll ask them a question, and they wind up taking you on some tangent while never really answering the question.

One more giveaway for an untruthful answer is the liar will generally repeat the exact sequence of the sentence being said. When asked, "Did you take the money?" A liar might reply "No, I did not take the money," where an honest person might respond, "Wasn't me", or What money?"

It's easy to spot a guilty person because of his defensive posture. When you see the person crossing his arms and making up a long explanation as to why he can't be the responsible party, you know there's more to the story. Blocking the body with objects such as a purse is also a sign of insecurity and anxiety for the potential liar.

Of course, a person exhibiting any of the above signs does not necessarily make him a liar. This is why it's important to know a person's true personality so you can use the above signs in comparison with baseline behavior to detect what is true and what is false.

The above pointers will help you in listening to others. But there's more to speech and tonality that professionals use with the power of persuasion. The next chapter will explain how you can use hypnotic language with the power of persuasion.

## Chapter 10
## How to Use Hypnotic Speech Patterns

Mentalists and marketers alike have a knack for getting you to think in certain ways and do certain things. As for marketers, they can get you to buy what they want you to buy.

While they call it a kind of hypnotic speech, it really doesn't make the person do something that goes against every fiber of their being. However, if you're on the edge, hypnotic speech will push you over to the side of acceptance.

Acceptance of what? Marketers can get you to buy their products; mentalists can get you to perform tricks such as picking the right card; and skilled politicians can get your vote.

The funny thing is that, as a victim of hypnotic persuasion, you do not believe you've been hypnotized at all. Conversely, you believe wholeheartedly that your choice is 100% *your* choice.

### *Tonality Secrets of Persuasion*

Conversational hypnosis is a performance art that can benefit those who are skilled in various ways. Remember, only 7% of what people understand from you actually comes from the words you're saying. Everything else has to do with body language and the tone of voice you're using – how you say what you say.

### Remembering the principles of speech delivery is important:

- Emphasis

Emphasis on certain words has a hypnotic effect in speaking. The same is true by the way in writing. For example, if I put emphasis on SPEECH TONE by capitalizing my words, you're more apt to remember that phrase in your subconscious mind.

Mentalists will emphasize certain words by speaking slightly more loudly or slowly to make sure the listener is aware. Often times the word of emphasis is spoken first. When you lean on a word, as if drawing it out, this is putting emphasis on that word. The emphasized word, when spoken, can literally change the meaning of an entire sentence.

For example, if you say, "Did *you* see her take the money?" emphasizing *you*, has a completely different meaning than "Did you see *her* take the money?" where the emphasis is on *her*. Still a different meaning is the sentence "Did you see her take the *money?*" emphasizing *money*.

- Speech Rhythm

Professional speakers who are trying to get a lasting point across often use rhythm. We repeatedly hear preachers or politicians speed up at times and then pause at certain words. This gives the listener a sense of wonder, as they wonder how the remainder of the sentence will go. As a listener, if you're hypnotized by the rhythm. Using a combination of rhythm and tonality in speaking is called trance rhythm, and it is used quite often among speakers. Trance inductions tend to pull in the listener; just as we enjoy listening to music, we subconsciously also enjoy listening to a speaker using the trance induction technique.

- Hypnotic Anchoring

The process of anchoring associates a behavior or hand motion with a particular state of mind. Similar to Pavlov's dog, our nervous systems are wired to elicit certain emotions when a repeated stimulus is elected. An example of this is a man at a funeral who is grieving over his deceased father. Someone comes up behind him unexpectedly and puts a hand on the man's shoulder to comfort him. However, this maneuver backfires when, some months later, someone again pats him on the back and he suddenly feels sad but does not know why. What's the missing link? The stimulus of the back patting anchored the sad state that the man had experienced. Once the anchor is in place, a simple pat on the back now elicits the same state of mind.

Of course, skilled hypnotists use this technique to elicit a positive result. Speakers often use it as a way to build confidence in speaking before large crowds. Get yourself in a happy and confident state of mind by thinking of a time you were at the top of your game. Then introduce a hand motion stimulus, something that's unique and is never done at other times. Rub your stomach; pat your head, or something completely unique when you're feeling extremely confident. Now, simply do that motion again before you speak in front of a crowd.

- Detached Statement Technique

This is a favorite technique among marketers and salespeople. This is a professional influential system. The pattern works by executing the following six steps:

1. Decide on which statements you want your prospect to accept.
2. The detached method is executed by developing a story to backup the statement.
3. Make sure that you own name is used in the story, establishing rapport with your prospect.
4. Use the stacking language pattern by reiterating other messages within the story. Now the same message is being quoted from multiple sources.
5. Be your own devil's advocate by questioning the statement. By doing this, others will be more open to agreeing with you rather than feeling the need to resist the statement.
6. Ask your prospect his opinion; "What do you think?"

- Pacing and Leading

Pacing and leading is a popular NLP tool that deals with influencing behavior by increased persuasive techniques. The method is often used in advertisements by leading the listener to believe you're speaking directly to him. Online marketers know that buyer conversions from click to sale are much higher in proportion when gearing the advertisement to a smaller niche target market.

In normal conversation, the pacing and leading technique is more difficult to recognize. It's obvious when you take a look at a hypnotist who gives suggestions, "You are breathing deeper now and you are feeling drowsy."

In a nutshell, pacing and leading in normal conversation has to do with subliminal suggestions following factual statements. You state the obvious, "you are breathing slowly," and then you suggest a new feeling, "you are feeling drowsy."

As a sales technique, the suggestion may go something like this:

*"We all know that growing a business is never easy. We have to be concerned with payroll and overhead, with a constant concern over making ends meet. But just imagine, what if there were a system in place to ensure that everything can run smoothly – something that can give you the benefit of peace of mind? Our coaching system will help you understand your business, resulting in greater cash flow and peace of mind."*

The sales pitch above used pacing with identifying the target market with the desperate need, and leading by introducing a suggested solution – the thing you want to sell.

- Bypass the Critical Factor

This is the technique of leading your subject from conscious to unconscious thoughts. While the conscious mind has only the ability to process 3-4 pieces of information per second, the unconscious is basically unlimited. This hypnotic technique is accomplished with the following steps:

1. Make sure you have complete attention from your subject.
2. The subject must be kept in an environment to ensure the experience is gratifying.
3. Speak as if in a trance, which facilities the subject to follow suit.
4. Maintain a hypnotic gaze eye contact; this builds rapport.
5. Add trance themes with hypnotic language– expressions of how you're feeling.
6. Use a hypnotic voice with a tone slightly slower and deeper than your usual voice.
7. Watch for signals on your subject that signify a trance such as changes in breathing or pupil dilation.

8. Be sure that the critical factor has been passed before making hypnotic suggestions, as the conscious mind will want to reject, but he unconscious mind will accept.

In normal conversation, the method of covert hypnosis brings out the attributes that the person already possesses.

For example, ask the person to describe an enjoyable experience. As they speak, take mental note of roughly four feelings they enjoy about the experience. How did things smell or feel in the experience? Now you have the ammunition you need to precede – you know what brings pleasure to your subject.

When proceeding with this hypnotic practice, you'll ask your prospect to remember feelings they experienced in the situation they had recalled. This is a technique taught in self-hypnosis where recalling enjoyable experiences can bring on a state of serenity. The newfound serenity can result in resolving problems that were once overwhelming.

- Tag question

This is a technique used in marketing as well as hypnosis. A statement is made, and followed up with a question to confirm that the person agrees. For example, a hypnotist might say, "If feels so good to relax, doesn't it?"

This technique is used to create the trance state where the subconscious mind is willing to accept the succeeding suggestion as statement of fact.

Marketers use this technique in advertisements all the time. They take you on a beautiful vacation in a luxurious car with children who are smiling and can do no wrong. This creates a beautiful feeling of desire within your subconscious. Then they pose the seductive question: "Wouldn't you rather have a Lexus?"

While it's good to know how to use hypnotic language on others, it's also advisable to be aware of how marketers are using it on us. Now that you have a basic acquaintance with the hypnotic language patterns used by professionals, you're better equipped to defend yourself against buying that which is actually not what your heart desires.

## Chapter 11
## Learning ESP

Extrasensory perception (ESP) is often misconceived as some sort of secret power available only to the gifted clairvoyants. Some even think the whole idea is ridiculous.

Hopefully, this chapter will give you a better understanding of exactly what ESP is and how you can tap into this kind of power.

*"Peace is a result of retraining your mind to process life as it is, rather than as you think it should be."* ... **Wayne Dyer**

Once we retrain our minds to process and accept life as it is, we are tapping into our natural ESP senses.

Yes, you read that right. Extrasensory perception is a skill that anyone can learn. We think that *extrasensory* relates to senses beyond the human norm. However, contrary to popular belief, ESP refers to the ability to tap into senses that are beyond normal *perception*.

Note the word *perception*; your ability to tap into sensations that are not perceived by the normal person does not mean that the person must possess certain psychic gifts. On the contrary, 90% of all sensory input of the normal human being is blocked. We are wired this way because, if we are aware of every piece of information fed to us, we would actually not be able perceive anything effectively. It would result in the inability to focus on the situation at hand.

Extrasensory perception is really only that – the ability to retrieve information by means other than the primary five senses. Those who are proficient in ESP have developed their minds with increased mind power by allowing the brain to tap into natural intuition. This unusual mind power enables people to influence situations important to them almost at will.

The only difference between the gifted ESP expert and the average person is that these people have chosen at an early age not to ignore their intuitions, but rather to cultivate those senses.

Those who have learned ESP have learned to expand their perception. In fact, children are often more in tune with seeing what appears to be supernatural because they are still in tune with their instincts from birth. The older we become, the more we tend to block out outside perceptions so as not to allow the mind to be interrupted from that on which we are concentrating. All we need to do is to learn how to wake up those suppressed senses.

Most of us have learned to suppress our ESP instincts because of the daily stresses to which we are subjected. As adults, our bodies are full of tension from the stress of daily life, which creates what psychologists call a noisy state of being. We all have internal dialog as we think thoughts. In the case of a stressed individual, those thoughts just won't shut up. The more we're preoccupied with tension from the outside world, the less we are able to awaken our senses to the ability of detecting more in the world around us.

We think that the world beyond most human conception is the illusion; however, the reverse is true. It's the preoccupied mind that blocks the universal power of creation that creates the illusion. That illusion is working against you because all you can see or think about is the pile of bills or the project that might not get completed in time.

ESP actually happens naturally when the mind is in a quiet and open state. It's the quiet and clear mind that can begin to manifest ESP effortlessly.

While the title of this chapter is *Learning ESP*, the actual method of developing ESP does not have to do with learning. We are all born with these skills; through the stress of daily living, we have hypnotized ourselves throughout our lives to ignore other senses.

Keep in mind, your brain has spent years of training to block out additional senses; you must now be patient in the process of dehypnotizing your brain so as to open your mind to new awareness.

## *The Process of Dehypnotizing:*

The first step is to learn to take all the chatter out of your brain – the emotional chatter caused from the stress of daily living. And, no, you don't have to move to the mountains and live like a monk.

Contrary to popular belief, you only need to focus about 10 minutes twice daily. Morning meditation exercises will put you in a state of awareness for the day where you are open to better ideas to work effectively. Evening meditation puts you in the proper state of mind for better sleep and recovery from daily stress.

## Proper meditation technique centers around three centers of being:

1. First is to pay attention to breathing.

While breathing is an involuntary bodily function, you can also control your breathing voluntarily. If you notice, forcing yourself to breath deeper and slower can actually reduce the stress you've feeling at any point in your day. Additionally, deep breathing has been discovered as a way to maximize focus just before entering a stressful situation.

Studies have shown that people who practice deep breathing exercises prior to interviews, tests, or athletic competitions are overall more successful in achieving their goal. The science behind this is that, under stress, we tend to breath shallow and fast, which actually decreases flow of oxygen to the body. As the body pulls less oxygen, your energy is depleted. As you decide to voluntarily practice deep and slower breathing prior to a stressful event, your focus is improved and anxiety is diminished. Less cortisol is released into the bloodstream.

In meditation, breathing is the first step. Breath in through your nose, counting to four as you inhale. Pay attention to the oxygen flowing in as your diaphragm raises. You will notice a more relaxed and focused feeling immediately. Exhale and out through your mouth, again to the count of four. After five to ten slowed breaths, you are now prepared to go to the second state of meditation.

   2.   Pay attention to body posture.

When in a state of meditation, the body must be postured to be relaxed enough to be comfortable, yet aware enough not to fall asleep.

The traditional meditation posture is to sit upright with legs crossed and fingers touching and palms up. However, most of us as beginners cannot achieve this posture for various reasons. If meditation is new to you, most likely this posture feels unnatural and very uncomfortable to you. Additionally, those of us with back trouble could feel a sense of back pain from trying to sit up straight for extended times.

Don't worry about it. As long as you are in a position that will not advocate falling asleep, sitting in a semi-upright position in an easy chair can achieve the same result. It is mandatory that you feel totally relaxed in order to allow your mind from transforming from the *beta* (awake) state to the *alpha* (deeper relaxed) state of meditation. Once in the alpha state, your mind is open to your natural intuition.

If sitting in a chair, make sure that your legs are not crossed so as to advocate complete relaxed leg muscles and even flow of oxygen throughout the bloodstream. While sitting in the traditional cross-legged position looks cool, it's most important to achieve a position that's right for you. Once your body is completely relaxed, it's time to focus your mind.

   3.   Pay attention to the state of your body, mind and spirit.

Keep your focus on your body, noticing the relaxed feeling from the toes up. You can concentrate on each section of your body, one muscle set a time. Focus on your toes and feet and how relaxed they feel. Work your way up on each section of the body until you're focusing on muscles around the eyes and forehead. Meditation practice can actually relieve headaches as well as other body pains affected by stress.

In fact, in addition to anxiety, studies have shown that regular meditation practice can manage symptoms associated with asthma, cancer, depression, insomnia, pain and high blood pressure.

Some people use a *guided meditation* technique, where you allow your mind to visit peaceful images to achieve better relaxation. With this method, try to remember your most relaxing places with all your senses – perhaps the smell of cookies as a child or the sound of the babbling brook you once visited on vacation.

For the purpose of allowing your mind to become more aware, *mindfulness meditation* is recommended. You can achieve this type of meditation by simply focusing on your relaxation experience during meditation, noticing how your body feels, concentrating on your breathing and feeling the oxygen entering your brain. As thoughts enter, let them go without judgment.

### *Achieving complete stillness is the beginning of achieving ESP.*

Be patient, as the process of dehypnotizing yourself to learn to tune out mind chatter of stressful living will take time. Imagine your body as a body of water with the ability to stay completely still, regardless of any pebbles or stones being thrown into the water.

Once you become proficient at mindfulness meditation, you'll notice that colors and sounds appear different as you gain a new perspective of the world around you. With enough practice, you will begin to see auras, hear thoughts, and detect spiritual solutions through ESP.

## Chapter 12
## The Important of Feedback in Learning Mentalism

While the forgoing tools in this book give you a lot to go on for learning the tricks to the trade for mentalists, it goes without saying that learning the art of mentalism takes much will, determination and practice to learn this skill successfully.

Furthermore, there is no way you can really be certain that what you've learned can be applied without some sort of feedback mechanism. Mentalism is not only the most impressive form of magic that can blow anyone's mind when done correctly; it is also the most difficult and time consuming to learn.

### *Be willing to fail.*

Naturally, like anything else, your first attempt at mentalist magic probably would not exhibit successful tricks. Being willing to stick your neck out regardless of possible demonstration of failure is a necessary ingredient for learning this type of skill. Keep in mind that most successful people find real success only one-step beyond an enormous failure.

*"I have not failed. I've just found 10,000 ways that won't work."...* **Thomas A. Edison**

It might help to watch some YouTube videos by some of the greats like Derren Brown or Uri Geller prior to practice. Note how presentation plays a big part in the believability of your trick.

Appearing cool, calm and confident lays the ground for the ability to pull of the power of mind control. Once you've learned a mentalist trick, practice in the mirror and pay attention to your hand gestures and facial expressions.

### *The following are simple mentalist magic tricks to practice:*

## 1. Card Trick – Pick Four

Allow the spectator to shuffle the card deck. Then, take the deck and pull a random card to show to spectator, making note that the cards are real. The appearance of looking for a random card to pull is only a show, as you're really checking out the bottom card. As you speak about there being no markings on the cards, this is a distraction to the spectator.

Then spread all the cards face down on the table and make sure you take note of where you put the final card which is the one for which you're aware. Say, "we're going to see how good your intuition is." Ask the spectator to pick three cards, one at a time.

For example, and say, "pick whichever card you believe is the 6 of hearts and slide it towards me." You know where the six of hearts is because this is the card you've witnessed from the bottom of the deck.

Then take a quick peek at the card, which is, most likely, not the card you know to be from the bottom. Then ask the spectator to pick another card (7 of hearts). The subject picks one and slides it to towards you, and you take a quick peek. Then ask the subject to pick up the king of clubs. That card is picked and you take a peek at it. You're peeking at all three cards, and not allowing the spectator to see.

It's important here to remember which cards are being picked. Now you're going to announce that you'll pick up the last card, at which time you say that you're picking a random card (king of diamonds). You announce that you'll be picking up a random card, but you're really picking the card you know.

Before you show the cards, ask the subject if they remember what the cards were, and before they answer, you tell them: and then name all the cards as you turn them over.

The trick to this is that you first ask the subject to pick the card you know where it is, and this is actually the card you're picking last. After you pick the last card, position it inconspicuously as the first one to be read. The spectator believes that *they* were the one who mysteriously picked that card. The first card named is actually the last one picked.

Most people cannot remember all four cards, but they will be impressed that the card they believed they picked up first was named first.

2. Mental shapes trick

This trick is performed in a comfortable atmosphere with about 20-25 inches between you and the spectator. Speak in a low, calm voice:

"Are you ready?" (Wait for response.) "Are you feeling mentally awake and alert?"

Then show approval with positive answer, "Great. Now, imagine there is a screen between us." As you speak, draw a rectangular figure with your pointer figures illustrating a screen.

Then say, "On that screen, I want you to project an image, like a square, but not a square." As you say that, your thumb and forefingers are forming the *illusion of a triangle* (not obviously touching, just creating a similar triangular illusion.)

What the spectator does not know is that you are subconsciously influencing the answer by using your hand gestures.

Now say, "Lock it in." Then continue, "Now project another shape and put that shape *around* the shape you've just created." As you speak the words "another shape, not a square," your hands are forming a partial circular motion. As you point to the back of your head and space between your eyes, command, "Now send me those images."

The fun part is the drama; "Yes, I'm starting to feel it now; it's a triangle inside a circle."

This is a fun way of using hand gestures and body language as an influential tool to give the illusion of mind reading.

3. Three of Diamonds

This trick requires only having the one card, the three of diamonds. Be sure to use distraction techniques to make your spectator continue to wonder about which card you're hiding rather than paying attention to your hand gestures. State that you will be mentally projecting to the spectator the identity of the card.

While you're making your quick hypnotic hand gestures, speak about how they need to guess the card, "Just think about the numbers and symbols down in the corner and up at the top, things down the middle."

Similar to the #2 trick above, you're making *diamond gestures* with your hands, which makes the spectator think of diamonds. You're using words like *low number* so that the spectator will pick a card in the range between 2 and 7. And the final hand gesture you're using puts *three* fingers in the center, which gives the hypnotic power of suggestion of a three to the spectator.

The hand gestures are quick, so as not to become too obvious that you're trying to implant thoughts in the spectator's mind.

In most cases, the spectator will say they are thinking about the three of diamonds, which, of course, is the card you're holding.

Be sure to get feedback from your spectator for continuous

improvement.

### *Why is feedback so important?*

It doesn't matter whether you succeed or fail at your earliest mentalist attempts. The point is to get feedback from your spectator, whether positive or negative.

Feedback is not only a necessity to perform magic tricks; it's also mandatory in the marketing world for those mentalist marketers who gain the power of persuasion over prospective customers.

Top companies have teams of analysts whose job is no more than to simply gather feedback from prospects and customers, tweak the ad, and test again. Effective feedback benefits everyone concerned – the marketer, the marketing company, the salesmen, customer, magician and spectator.

The following reasons of why feedback is so important will give you proper perspective on how good feedback can benefit a wide variety of stakeholders.

1.  Feedback is always available.

While many companies issue surveys to get customer's feedback for the purpose of improvement, the mentalist can get feedback he needs by only simply being aware. Take note of the person's expressions and body language. If they appear surprised and interested, you're on a winning streak.

2.  Feedback encourages better listening.

As an aspiring mentalist, it's critical to become the best listener you can be. When people respond to your trick, be sure you understand their response, whether positive or negative. Give a satisfying answer to ensure them that they have been understood.

3. Feedback is motivating.

In the world of business, feedback can motivate better performance among employees. When people are asked to provide feedback, they feel important and therefore are more likely to come forth with good business decisions with their heart behind the business.

4. Feedback improves overall performance.

Whether positive or negative, feedback will alter the mentalist's abilities for a better performance the next time around. Sometimes negative feedback such as constructive criticism can actually be even more beneficial.

5. Continuous feedback equals continuous learning.

As we are aware of the feedback of our performance, we strive for improvement. And, if we improve upon our skill each day, even if just to the slightest degree, we will eventually become extremely proficient. It's the very reason why major companies employ entire departments responsible for detecting feedback.

The combination of practice with proper feedback on a continuous basis is the foundation for becoming a successful mentalist. And, even if your only goal is to become better aware and therefore gain better control of your life, you are on the road to success.

A continuous review of the pointers in this book, coupled with continuous practice and feedback, will bring you a happier and more fulfilling life.

## About the Author

Stefan Cain has spent the majority of his working career in numerous academic research positions, working on a wealth of psychological, societal and cultural topics. His research work and adept studies have been used to form the backbone of many popular titles available today, providing him with the experience and hunger to delve deeper into some avenues of thought.

Alongside his serious academic work, Stefan has been published in a number of prominent publications; filing news reports, features and insightful opinion pieces on myriad topics throughout his career. It was here, in this capacity as a journalist, that he first began to start writing about human behavior.